When We Are Kites

poems by

Barbara Jacksha

Printed in the United States of America
by Amazon KDP

ISBN (paperback version): 978-0-9987121-5-4

Cooper Brandberg Publishing
Santa Fe, NM 87508

Front cover art: iStockphoto | LUMEZIA
Interior art: iStockphoto | Dmitry Zyrin

Dedicated
to all those
moments
of courage
and grace
that find us

Contents

Thermal Lift

Aloft

Cliff's Edge

voices ride the wind
of the abyss, reminding us
we are *more*

Somewhere Underneath

Today you remember
to remove
the heavy, matted oak leaves
you packed over
tender roots
to protect them
from winter ice.

You remove the layers
brought in by the wind:
obligations,
expectations
piled on
blocking the sun.

Today you remember,
your hands remember
how to pull back the weight
and let light pour over
what is already beginning
to sprout.

Dawn Sky Offers Her Choices

the Sangre de Cristo mountains
reveal two sets of clouds—
one, a stretch of impenetrable gray,
a battleship shrouding rocky peaks.

above the shadow,
feathery wisps
of teal and raspberry pink,
long arms open
and reaching…

dawn catches my gaze,
whispers
You choose.
You choose.

Getting to Know the Light

When your chubby fingers
stack blocks in slanted beams
of afternoon sun,
you learn the game
light plays with shadow—
ducking into darkness,
then sparking bright.

Maybe you hear
sighs of future moments
drifting in
like motes of dust,
or a lullaby,
or the soft scuff
of a ballerina's
well-worn shoes
twirling you toward
a path you'll someday discover.

When you do, you'll learn
the sacred burn
when light blinds,
the desperate void it leaves
when it seems to drop from sight,
snatching your stuttering heart
and scrambling your senses.

Even then, within you,
the twirling dance continues—
the ballerina,
poised on pointe,
testing her limits,
inviting you to join her
on the head of the pin
each moment provides,
where you can always
find the light.

Tipping Point

one foot
before the other,
this life:
a tightrope.
harder
when legs
don't listen
anymore

edges blur
when eyes fail,
boundaries
of light and shadow
worn by an eroding wind
while the great black bear
paces below

one foot
before the other
until light embraces shadow
the great black bear
gleams with light
and the fear of falling
becomes the grace
of letting go

How I Wore Them

This is the way I remember
the rain boots my mother bought me:
tall, black, rubbery,
stiff shutter-like buckles
that sealed me
tight
against rain.

This is the way I wore those galoshes:
embarrassed
at the slapping, flapping
clown-foot way
they climbed school bus steps
while my classmates
giggled and stared.

This is the way
I kept wearing those galoshes:
fearful
of rain,
choosing
the dry, the safe
while life slipped exotic invitations
under my door.

This is the way I remove my galoshes:
I flip open the shutters one by one.

My barest feet slip out
into sharp cool rain
into unexpected puddles
that disappear by dawn.
My feet,
eager to splash—
leave prints in the rain.

At Nest Fall

we are curious birds, chittering
a half-known tune,
ruffling neon feathers—
one foot clutching
a nest already falling
to sharp wind,
one foot feeling into
empty air

golden dawn
splits the day open,
feeds our old trophies
to the breeze
while dew
reweaves us
into the liminal glass
of stars

at nest fall
we lift our heads
extend our wings
offer the twig we cherish most
to our emergent space
already swirling
already forming
in ascending air

Blue Chalcedony in Four Parts

Like ice, you slipped from my hand—
split on tile floor
into four pieces, clean breaks
I could have glued

You said:
No, please don't

You become
that Revolutionary
cartoon, the snake
with disjointed parts:
Join or Die—a call for unity
you'd already answered
before setting yourself free

You remain,
four pieces of a puzzle
to arrange and rearrange
liberated
from the yoke
of a single solution,
now inviting me to join
the breathless momentum
of always becoming
something new

All It Took

one key,
tarnished
by the breath
of people
who believed they knew
what was best
for me

this key,
fitted to
a single locked door
lost within
my misaligned heart
waiting
to recognize itself
again

just one key,
one turn,
one step through
that doorway

reuniting me
with myself

I Am Not Your Door

Do you see my door—
the green-painted stripes
and mandarin-wrapped bells?

Do you hear the rattle
of seed pods and tender branches
given me by sparrows and wrens?

Do you feel the precious heat
of all the heartbeats warming space
within these walls?

   Please don't mistake my door for yours.

   My door cannot open for you.
   No matter how long you knock.

Your singular door is out there,
the doorway to all your hidden treasure
already swinging wide to welcome you in.

Initiate Cartography

After the call,
when I asked *where*,
her sparrow voice
echoed still mountains,
laid rock cairns—
scattered, random runes
mapping possible pathways.
    She said:
    Begin and end beneath my stars
    and dance the stars within.

When I asked *what*,
she traced
my tattoo-lined palms,
my feet, flat prairies
laden with gold, stale stalks,
hungry
for the release of harvest.
    She said:
    Listen to the wind-blown coins of my
    aspen speaking in golden tongues.

When I asked *how*,
she rolled tides
across my body, her inland sea;

I swam toward jagged shores,
heard harbor bells,
sensed warm berths
waiting within the fog.
    She said:
    Ride my heaves and howls, my seals'
    laughter, the breathy breach of my whales.

My heart spoke quiet thunder.
I asked, *why me*?
She raised amazonite eyes,
teal bands of
grass and lagoon,
forest and sky,
and within them,
twin sparrow eggs.
    She said:
    How could it not be you?

Crosswinds

buffeted by gales
we balance
we turn

High Wire

Patricia dusts to gospel
hips swaying to the beat;
she scrubs for Jesus
banishes negative thoughts
down the drain.
she says, I'm not tired yet

but I am

roasting in a hot
desert afternoon
riffs spark on my skin,
like lightning
on the high wire
where a mass choir sings praise
and all I can think of
is whether grasping
that high wire
would char my hands
or finally
lead me
to my true
name

Between Light

I cannot wake the six-toed cat,
padding floors
to the purring cadence
of hush and breath,
while my sleep
wanders, a snake
loosening its skin,
eluding the ropes
between hours

I would change my name,
apologize to trees,
pick shards of night
from the grass,
beg a pardon
for the insurrection of owls
my sleep has become

Who can rest
in the hours of the wolf,
the time of a single floating
light: that moon beacon
pressing the ticking clock
of no time
toward morning's
changing prism of sight—

while the owls
claim their branches,
ruffling feathers
into echoes
that haunt the hours
of fragile day

3 p.m.

this day—
a shifting chameleon's path:
    determined to forgetting
    inspired to why-bothering
and one infuriating question:
    why is it
    I still can't pull
    gleaming coins
    from behind my ear?

This feeling—
so-so, iffy, meh, blah
    fries without salt
    toast without butter
tempted
by the witch under the stairs
inviting me to forget myself, nap
    soft, squishy, sugary
    melty by the fire
where I can read *Vogue* backwards
until Mercury goes direct
and the Equinox
shuts the door on this
blackboard-scratching day
of bone-bending
uncertainty

How You Can Approach the Sky

I see you on the fence,
looking skyward while
juggling precious objects,
exhaling bright, chromatic sighs

Before you offer yourself
as supplicant to the sky,
kite down her dreamy memoir,
read everything she's told the sea—
tales fanciful and caustic
and ridiculously true

Embrace a silent conversation—
language creates
bumbling expectations
and shuddering perceptions
aching to fly themselves free

Watch how buoyant balloons
and street musicians
offer their questions upward,
honoring Sky's curious clouds,
her capricious, restless breeze

Forget about beginner's mind—
do not come to Sky empty.

Fill her
with all your heartbreaks,
misgivings and joys

Above all,
be patient.
Sky tattoos her own,
with rainbow flourish,
in her own time

My True Name

My true name is uncertainty
hammered by headlines,
an unknown soldier in a
war of hate-flung words

My true name is incongruity
angry at drought's wind-whipped siege
while loving this land
with her fields of resilient wildflowers
and protective cactus thorns

My true name is conjecture
wondering which beloved bird will fly home next
I skip stones over my to-do list,
adult longing
to be child again

My true name is anthem
singing loud, no doubt
raspy and off-key,
regretting only the songs
I once kept chained
behind rows of brittle teeth

Unraveling

I have fallen apart like a nest,
bent twigs
and downy feathers
yielding to gravity.
Memories
of eggs once laid,
drift like a pile of leaves—
accepting
the end of their season,
anticipating
the bite of a winter wind.

In falling apart, I have reached
for comfort food
and fortune-cookie answers.

Sometimes
like the copper-haired heroine
on the cover of a romance novel,
I've reached for the hero, the savior, the man.
Sometimes
I've reached for the mercy of my apartment walls,
for the scripture of Hallmark TV or the God
I was taught to pray to, who didn't answer
in a telegram-from-heaven way
that I could understand.

Now I fall apart on purpose,
pulling the orange thread
on the sweater my mother
swaddled me in for warmth
and safe anonymity,
and as I pull I wonder
what will fall out first—

        an old china teacup
        saved for special occasions,
        my sludgy certainty
        that I was never strong,
        all those laughter-filled days
        I'd hoped could be reborn,
        the old dog tags of loves
        that will never be gone.

As I fall apart, I wonder
whether I should save these things,
save the yarn dropping around me,
preserve it
for the next sweater I will weave,

but it is hard to grab anything
when you discover you are wind
and an unexpected January thaw.
That you pulse with the hearts
around you, within you,
in a perfect rhythm of love and care.

And you know:

    you are warmer without the sweater,
    safer when unconfined,
    braver with the whole world facing you down,
and you can embrace jittering unknowns
as blank sheets of paper
emerging in front of you
when you are more ready than ever
to dream your new poems.

Firewalk (when there's nothing left to do)

Hop, skip, jump
the path of insanity.

Kick your shoes off,
burn your toes,
roast your fingers,
scorch some of that precious hair.

Stupid path.
Don't turn away.

Firewalk the insanity.
You can do it.
Everyone is watching
& nobody cares.

Eat pineapple while you walk.
Charred pineapple is delicious.
Insanely sweet.
As are you,
sweeter with each step,
your flesh
fading to ash.

Insanity declares
you're up next
for the big reveal.

& there you go,
a greedy gusto of flame.
Insanity
giggles and grunts
like a pig,
then wallows
in your ashes
to claim you.

But I see you,
sneaky phoenix—
you've already sparked on
fierce, pyro-synced wings.

Bless the Uncertain

sometimes I balance
atop my beliefs,
those sharp, thin pins
piercing my feet
while my arms flail,
and I pray
faith will hold me steady
as my certainty
digs in deep

sometimes I forget to pray
for a broader presence
to pluck me with its eagle feet,
drop me in that swift, singing river
that welcomes jagged rocks,
the bones of waterlogged trees—
drop me there
where I can swim and drown,
my pockets weighted
with all I thought I knew

then may I rise,
a newborn whale
breaching the surface
offering a poem, a touch,
a singular breath to the sky

there may I dive
again and again—
each fathom
a knowing
deeper
clearer
than
the
last

Everything In Its Place

somewhere
all my lost trains of thought
pull into their home stations,
warm, covered berths
waiting at a long journey's end

somewhere
all my missing socks
keep forgotten dreams snug and warm,
and give new seeds a cozy, safe place
to grow

somewhere
all those lost keys
receive payment due
for keeping me searching,
keeping me
where I needed to be
at exactly the right time

somewhere
the woman
my child self wanted to be
prepares tea and scones
to celebrate my courage
for becoming so much more

The Geometry of Daydreams

safeguard your sacred visions,
the piercing clarities that shatter
mirrors placed
so you would doubt
what you see

do not give even a sample
for testing—
skeptical analysts
cannot track the intonation
of your bones.
They will measure and weigh,
dissect your thoughts:
        points and lines,
        shapes and sizes,
        solids and altitudinal schematics,
as if they could comprehend
the essence your delicate
spider web vision reveals

you alone know
how to absorb your visions,
how to follow them inward
to the abstract alchemies
spun out each day

in the intricate language
of your time-pulsed heart
already spinning threads
already spinning tomorrow

(Mis)understanding

Hi, It's me…

Sorry I haven't said much lately.
I've been busy misunderstanding Grace,
expecting to summon her with
offerings of guilt and gold,
drifting incense,
and desperate midnight prayers.
But Grace, it seems, prefers
lobbing lopsided dinner rolls,
and shaking lyrics out of lilacs.
She's especially fond
of standing under train trestles
speckled, freckled with age
that belong to pigeons
and mice that fly
when no one is watching
except Grace,
who always sneaks in
unexpectedly
with
ambrosia wine,
sandwiches,
and succulent,
heart-sparking advice

Thermal Lift

within surrender
we ride
invisible currents

Fragile Ground

Bravery draws you to Tucson—
your ragged edges
melt into the desert
that erases
paved roads
and your advancing footprints

Bravery echoes—
the saguaros
wave thick arms,
motion you cannot see

while you follow faint trails,
protecting cryptobiotic
expanses,
waiting for beetles,
snakes, and lizards
to cross before you,
skittering onto land
too fragile
for your uncertain feet

You enter cautiously,
feel the saguaros
hold the air open for you,
all these lands
foreign,

yet the dusty scent
familiar on your tongue
like you roamed here
in a distant life
tipping your hat
or flicking your lizard tail

at those about to realize—
the courage they seek
is the bravery
that already
compelled them
to enter

How We Live the Answered Heart

We exhale questions,
float them like morning mist
toward a distant land.

Questions are the paradox
of chirping chicks
arriving before their eggs.
They shuffle us
over a familiar, thorny path,
blind us to the forest of answers
lived without question by
    badgers,
    king snakes,
    and whales.

Like them, we are answers,
undivided.

Questions spin from the mind,
shards broken away
by a relentless wind.
Answers blossom unbidden,
in any season,
fragrant fruits of our transformation—

    Love translating itself,
    one answered heart at a time.

Between

Making tea,
I falter on solid ground,
watch my tea slosh a jig
against its rim
as though it danced
in someone else's hands.

Within this tiled floor,
a new surface cups my feet.
I walk with it,
ride its bobbing current,
remembering water,
and the tireless
pulsing sway of kelp
along a gentle shore.

My steps become
a Tai Chi walk—
slow,
waving hands like clouds,
offering salutations
to this new world
forming
on the weathered bones
already giving way.

Unbound from worry and hurry,
my shoulders sink,
breath softens.
I drop
into the space and pace,
the gentle currents carved
by the deep song of whales.

I become
like the single stone resting in a stream,
no longer recognizing
the white-water frenzy
rushing over me.
Present and still,
I no longer wonder
which experience
of solid ground
is real.

Consider This

It is possible to be
a twirling mote of dust
kicked up by a dog—welcomed
through an open window,
then woven
into confident threads of sunlight

It is possible to be
one note of a warbler's call
lifted then swirled back
to grace the throat that sang it

It is possible to be
a singular word
picked from a poet's page
or a bright graffiti wall,
one word held in the mouth,
juicier than pomegranate or pear

It is possible to be
that moment you bite down,
the moment you let juice dribble
down your chin,
and you are reborn,
a babe with fresh-blinking eyes
taking in each small miracle
for another first time

Circles of Motion

motion loops
the bee's invisible, honey-mapped path,
an airplane's glinting silver roar,
the waltz
of each in-breath of life
and its inevitable exhale

even straight lines:
spirals twisting,
beginning to end,
and beginning again,
a Mobius path
to the pure heart in all things

the flutter of a feather
on the lawn, offered
in quiet grace
by its maker
finds new life on my altar—
a prayer for beauty,
for release and fresh turnings,
for indomitable life

The Names We Are We Become

Have you seen
this chimeric underground—
painted roses serenading,
lavender ducks
commanding their cellos,
ballooning into fretful people
just for a day, a trickster
day that seems to last
forever, even
as jaguars gather chanterelles
and hens lay eggs
on dream-lit pillows.

We need not fear
this waking from false day,
one as false and true
as the next.
We stretch into fractal-blue
morning or night
our breath tones
piercing the chill,
mixing under with above,
guiding star-slips
that sow mountaintops
like water lotus blooms.

We will remember

our secret, braided names,
our wildest chimera
building her impossible nest
even among thorns,
her comfort,
this rumbling hum,
this liminal
burst of blueberry,
this authentic dawn.

After the Namings

I could tell you the stories
of bear becoming stone,
stone carving bear,
comet birthing bear,
mouth opening comet,
comet shedding stone,
bear chasing comet

The stories of stone
absorbing comet tales,
comets cracking open,
hatching bears
into hungry mouths

no longer mouth

or comet

or stone

or any other
imagining

Let us play
within the things
that have shed their names

Let us be
un-named
un-beared
un-stoned
un-cometed
un-mouthed

Let us discover
what becomes
within the remains of names

All Things Seen

All things seen depend on eyes transmitting to brain,
brain translating impulse, the electricity
of neurons and quarks and bits of magic
impossible to perceive

All magic depends on belief, on knowing
what you see is just the dream,
intention bled into being
when you came here with your faithful, beating heart

All your faith depends on scaling a cliff, knowing
you cling to atoms made largely of air
crafted somewhere in this astonishing universe
only temporarily real

All your knowing of reality, bundled
in the single stone you skip on a calm pond,
in the frog who doesn't mind the disturbance, his eyes
blinking in bright sun before he dives to the murkiest
of bottoms:
        where the stone settled,
        where your faith sent the stone to reside,
        where the lack of illumination
        only makes reality easier to see

Witches' Dream

On rocky, barren shore, one
twisted tree where none belongs
        Spirit Tree to Ojibwe
        Witch Tree to trappers, voyageurs.
No one knows her age.
Sere and shrunken, roots
still splitting glacial stone.

November breathes ice,
witch limbs tremble.
I shiver with her, see
        hardened breasts
        bone-thrust hips
        reedy, rippled thighs.
Prickly fingers white with
moss or frost point skyward.
She leans toward water—
one day she will dive.

That night twig fingers slip
her dream to mine. I see
        light shimmers
        like rare white bats
        skimming restless waves—
        the hag daughter's reflection.

Crone hands stir wind

rise to tap
the daughter's round radiant face.
Witch needles rustle, whisper—
    Remember where you came from

Raven flies, arrow through light.
Silver-moon voice cackles back
    Always

When We Are Kites

When we remember
we are kites,
carrying sunsets
on our shoulders
we know
the crisp apple tang
of a season ready to fall

We know
the ledge will always find us
when we are ready,
the next great leap
loosening our fingers,
uncurling our toes
from around a granite threshold
already letting go

When we are kites,
we know the breeze
that carries us
into dense fog
and unmappable shadows,
toward the river of light
we are certain
still flows below

We learn
to trust the thermals,
the breathless lifts,
the aching turns,
those moments of blinding sun
that burn away
any lingering desire
to cling
to crumbling cliffs
or hide
in safe, unremarkable
sight

Blackberry Moon

I'm discovered by the moon, peeling blackberries
into butterflies, and within a breath this moon tries to tweak

the recipe my mother gave me, insisting
berries lack skin, that juice pools in place

by intention and phantom gravitational forces
overseen by crickets and nameless night birds,

but I have watched blackberries shed their skins,
bathe in moonlight until dawn wanders by

and we are amnesiacs again, forgetting all secret flavors,
stuffing blackberries into pies, not remembering

to count the many ticklish layers
of our own enchanted skin

Worlds Within World (a blitz poem variation)

We are beyond us
We are worlds
Worlds have no anthems
Worlds pledge allegiance
Allegiance to grace and fortitude
Allegiance to bright futures and slow-swimming swans
Swans fly the distance
Swans swim synchronistically
Synchronistically, we invent time for our love of clocks
Synchronistically, we wind clocks to jar our memory
Memory waits for no one
Memory of the worlds we are
Are tasting like first snowflakes on the tongue
Are buzzing like honeybees around lemonade
Lemonade distills many worlds under gods
Lemonade passes between neighbors
Neighbors, people just thresholds away from us
Neighbors, we remember to call friends
Friends unite through hand-written letters
Friends toast harmony and chocolate
Chocolate swirls worlds together
Chocolate soothes wounds with caramel
Caramel heals gaps between lovers
Caramel gives the gods something to sink their teeth into
Into our business, they press
Into our hearts, they leave gifts we remember
Remember stories we've ignored or forgotten
Remember wise words we've never believed

Believed were possible
Believed anything was possible
Possible that someone new would fix our worlds
Possible that we mistake our worlds as other
Other, beyond our skins
Other, downcast eyes and frowns
Frowns are forgetful
Frowns look outward not inward
Inward, where frowns were voted down
Inward, where frowns were recycled into blackberry thorns
Thorns with spiny purpose
Thorns we can accept
Accept that drop of blood
Accept that we bleed in this life
Life, marching as if it had somewhere to go
Life, tumbling in a puff of breeze in the end
End as we began
End, seeding secrets that elevate worlds
Worlds within worlds
Worlds teasing us wild and wise
Worlds
Wise

When You Do

When you know yourself
as senses in motion,
gathering:
the shadow of a raven overhead,
a dog's cold nose on your hand,
wind rattling the pines,
a cool sleek pane of glass,
the first scent of rain

When you know yourself
as a mapmaker,
sensing hidden paths
between distant points,
luring out the lost connections
and blazing new ones
that startle and delight you

Then poetry will join you:
an oddly shaped leaf
bouncing atop a determined ant,
the raven that returns
to your pine tree every evening,
the wayward tarantula strolling
through your kitchen,
a thousand other tiny things,
moments of meaning
you'd never notice,
you'd never expect—

until you do

When You Are Love

When you are love, you live this world
as a bee attunes to flowers,

you know
the wildflowers that offer the sweetest pollen
that you can carry back to feed your colony.

And you know the other plants
that will not sustain you, yet you enter them
willingly, your body shedding its coat
of precious pollen where it might land unseen

a selfless gift—
    of vital sun-kissed grains
    of sustenance
    of love becoming more

Aloft

in bright moments
our scattered selves
remember

You Already Know

I can't tell you how I remember—
my dogs gobbled up yesterday,
licked out its caramel center
leaving the rind behind
for the birds

I can't tell you how I know—
fate swept away all the foghorns
leaving ticket stubs, flecks of
birdseed and traces of fancy
Elvish script you can only read
while dangling upside down

I can't exactly explain—
I'm busy squeezing bagpipes,
building a rainforest for butterflies
so they'll stop scratching up the sky

I can't tell you what you need—
life left you a crock of
magic mac and cheese.
Open the lid,
dive in with both hands,
squeeze the gooey chunks
and then we'll talk

Traces

When we arrived, we chose our wild skins.
Mine, fair, nearly translucent, revealing
white tendons intertwined
with thin blue vessels,
a steady course for blood
ferrying its gentle heat.

I've watched the sun coax freckles
from winter hiding—
girl-leopard spots
I connected with imaginary lines,
shaping myself
into constellations
and the faces of those
traveling
this life inside me.

When I return, I will shed all I've worn,
spread the freckled skin before a new sun,
an offering,
my imagined tracings
mirroring the constellations above,
while I recognize the faces
I drew as those who come to welcome me,
those who have waited my lifetime
for my return.

Indivisibility

I am not my 66 years
nor the 39 days before my birthday,
not the 1 man I've married,
or the 43 years and 8 dogs
we've shared.

I am not a multiple of 8
or the square root of 7 or 9.
I am not the star-lit expanse
from Earth to Moon,
nor the 20 yards to the end
of my driveway.

I am not the 1 you see
or the 1 spotted in the mirror.
I am not 2 eyes or ears,
the dozens of restless organs,
or the 10 fingers
strumming an autumn wind.

I am the 1 spark always hidden.
Not simply a prime number,
a magic number,
a complex number.
I am 1 like my friend Pi,
an irrational number
counting up,
an infinite number

counting down—
indivisible
by death's
inching shadow
or life's
perpetual
current
of grateful
sighs.

In Paradise with Master Mun

the grotto welcomes our return—
cool damp air paints
my lips
sweet
with jasmine and orange
while moisture
seeps from stone,
drips
to a small carved basin
where three large koi,
pomegranate and white,
hang in a trance—
their fins,
a faint, occasional
flutter.

I ask why
in paradise,
fish would be confined
to so small a space.

Master Mun smiles.

they are here of their own choosing,

perhaps they seek privacy, or the taste of fresh minerals,
or they wish to commune with this water or this stone.

tomorrow they may swim a fast-running stream
or bathe in a warm shallow lake. that is their choice as well.

my choices reverberate—

why am I here?

why now?

where will I be tomorrow?

do not assume that the world you leave for sleep
need be the one you wake to. like the koi, you too may dream
a new dream.

fragrant blossoms fall to water,

of no concern to the koi;

my reflection

in petal-drawn ripples

begins its grand journey

outward.

an eager tail flicks

water dances to new life—

a door swings open

I Am and Then I'm Not

There are days
I cannot bend
beneath one more vaulted ceiling,
or feel the crush
of artfully adorned walls

There are days
I cannot bear the burn
of one more jaded conversation—
politics or money or the many ills
that befall us all

There are heartbeats
when I know I am an egret
slipping
through fertile layered realities,
living countless lives
as fully as this

No surprise
that I am here
and not,
blinking
back and forth
within each breath,
soaring,
then splashing puddles

In this beat,
if you want to find me,

I am riding a dragon.

I am standing in the rain.

About the Author

Barbara Jacksha is a poet and fiction writer whose work often explores the mysteries of the spiritual and natural world, the intersection of the small and the ordinary with the phenomenal.

Barbara is the author of *We All Live Here,* a book of poems celebrating our kinship with animals. Her poetry and short fiction have been published in *Mindprints, Talking Stick, Beloit Fiction Journal, The Summerset Review, Mad Hatter's Review,* and virtualwriters.org. Her work has been nominated for the Pushcart Prize and appears in the W.W. Norton anthology *Flash Fiction Forward.*

Barbara lives near Santa Fe, New Mexico with her husband and shaggy wonder-dog. She shares this magical setting with wandering bobcats and badgers, prairie dogs and rabbits, an ever-changing chorus of birds, and several neighborhood coyotes.

You can visit Barbara's website at www.barbarajacksha.com. Don't miss her *Radiant Authenticity* blog, which celebrates the profound nature of this life's journey.

Acknowledgements

Earlier versions of some of these poems were published in previous years. My gratitude goes out to these journals and organizations, as well as their readers.

- “Witches’ Dream,” in *Talking Stick*
- “In Paradise with Master Mun,” in *Vox*
- “High Wire,” on *virtualwriters.org*
- “All Things Seen” and “My True Name,” in *Tiferet Journal* workshop participant collection

Acknowledgments

www.ingramcontent.com/pod-product-compliance
Lightning Source LLC
LaVergne TN
LVHW010841120826
845149LV00020B/3421

* 9 7 8 0 9 9 8 7 1 2 1 5 4 *